NIC BISHOP
FROGS

Written and photographed by
Nic Bishop

Sch

There are more than 5,000 different kinds of frogs. Scientists are discovering new ones every year.

Some frogs look like moss.

Others are see-through.

A few frogs even glide through the air.

Frogs have large eyes, long back legs, and amazing, damp, stretchy skin. They do not drink like you do. They absorb water through their skin instead.

Frogs can breathe through their skin, too, but only if their skin stays moist. That is why most frogs live in rainy or damp places.

Like other toads,
spadefoot toads
are a kind of frog.
They stay damp
by spending much
of their lives
underground. They
come to the surface
after it rains.

Red-eyed tree frogs live in rain forest trees. They have special suckers on their toes that cling to leaves.

Bullfrogs, and many other kinds of frogs, live near ponds. You will hear them calling to their mates in spring. They lay their eggs in ponds, too.

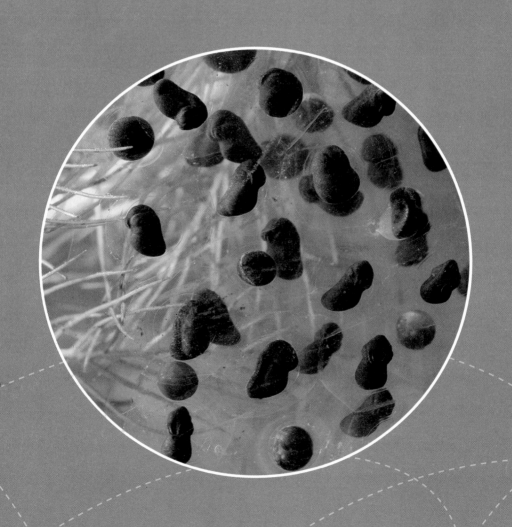

These eggs hatch into tadpoles, which eat tiny plants and animals.

As a tadpole gets older, it grows legs and its tail disappears.

One day, the baby frog is ready
to hop out of the pond.

Frogs love to eat. Their large eyes spot anything that moves. Then they snap it up with their sticky tongues.

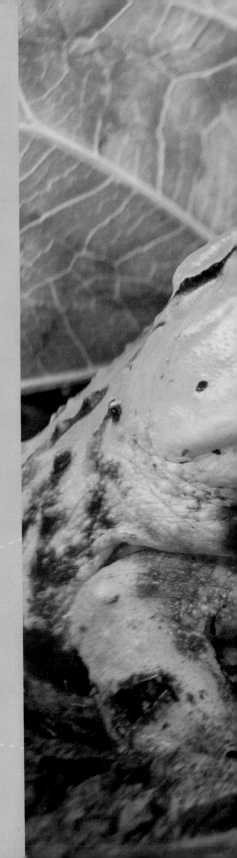

Most frogs eat insects. But the horned frog eats almost anything it can fit in its big mouth. It even eats mice.

Frogs are always watching out for danger. Birds, snakes, and even other frogs may eat them.

Dart poison frogs stay safe because they have *toxic* skin. *Predators* leave them alone.

Many other frogs keep very still
and hope not to be noticed. Even
if they are spotted, they can
leap to safety.

If a frog stays safe, it may live several years.

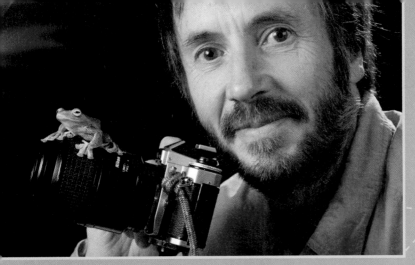

A Closer Look
with Nic Bishop

Frogs are *amphibians*, which means "leading two lives."
Most live in water when young and on land as adults.
They are found on every continent except Antarctica.
The biggest, the Goliath frog from Africa, is as heavy as
a newborn baby. One of the smallest, the gold frog from
South America, could sit on the top of your little finger.

To take the photographs for this book, I raised some
frogs at home, caring for them as they grew from tadpoles.
A few, like the gliding frogs, are now favorite pets. They
wake me some nights with their gentle singing. I found
other frogs by exploring the ponds and swamps near my
home. I also visited rain forests, where I was amazed by
the many colors of dart poison frogs, as tiny as jelly beans
on the ground! My favorite, though, was the glass frog.
It was as small as a pea, with thin legs and delicate toes.
You can see it on page 3 of this book.

Glossary

amphibians: a class of animals that usually has gills and lives in water when young, and breathes air and lives on land when adult

predators: animals that live by hunting other animals for food

toxic: having a poisonous effect

Photo Index

strawberry dart poison frog,
page 1

mossy frog,
page 2

glass frog,
page 3

gliding frog,
pages 4–5, back cover

wood frog,
pages 6–7

young African bullfrog,
pages 8–9

spadefoot toad,
pages 10–11

red-eyed tree frog,
pages 12–13, front cover

American bullfrog,
page 14

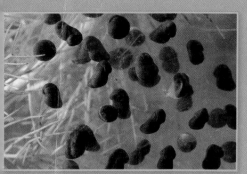

American bullfrog eggs,
page 15

American bullfrog tadpole,
pages 16–17

American bullfrogs,
pages 18–19

young African bullfrog,
pages 20, 21, 29

horned frog,
pages 22–23

dart poison frog,
pages 24–25

American bullfrog,
pages 26–27

African bullfrog,
page 32

ISBN 978-0-545-60570-0

12 11 10 9 8 7 6 5 4 3 2 1   15 16 17 18 19 20/0

Printed in the U.S.A. 40
First printing, January 2015